THE NIGHT WATCHES

THE NIGHT WATCHES

BY

JASON W. JOHNSON

Brewer Publishing   Searcy, Arkansas   2023

PUBLISHED BY BREWER PUBLISHING

Copyright © 2023 by Jason Johnson

All rights reserved. In accordance with the U.S. Copyright Act of 1976, the scanning, uploading, and electronic sharing of any part of this book without the permission of the publisher constitute unlawful piracy and theft of the author's intellectual property. If you would like to use material from the book (other than for review purposes), prior written permission must be obtained by contacting the publisher at brewerpublishing@gmail.com. Thank you for your support of the author's rights. The publisher is not responsible for websites (or their content) that are not owned by the publisher.

https://www.brewerpublishing.net/

The colophon is a trademark of Brewer Publishing.

Library of Congress Cataloging-in-Publication Data

Johnson, Jason W., b. 1975

The night watches : poems / by Jason W. Johnson. – 1st ed.

p.   cm.

ISBN: 979-8-218-16011-1

I. Title.

2023933772

https://lccn.loc.gov/2023933772

Manufactured in the United States of America

First Edition

In memory of my father.

CONTENTS

	Foreword	*xi*
	Acknowledgments	*xix*
	Editor's Note	*xxi*
I.	The Night Watches An Ascent	1
II.	Anthems for Advent	27
III.	Hymns from Purgatory	41
IV.	CV A Sentence for Pentecost	59
	Note About the Author	73
	Note About the Type / Credits	74

FOREWORD

In his new collection, *The Night Watches*, Jason Johnson delves into the theme of divine revelation and its significance in contemporary society. Through his use of language and imagery, he explores the struggle to understand and connect with "an un- elixired be- yond" in a world where love and faith have become scarce. *The Night Watches*, like all of Johnson's work, is an intense examination of the search for meaning and purpose in an uncertain world. In his poetry, God is never portrayed as a straightforward or simplistic concept, but rather as a complex and challenging force that requires perpetual effort and perseverance to understand. Thus, both introspection and extrospection are evident in Johnson's poems. In fact, an overall survey of Johnson's larger body of work shows a deep interest in subjectivity and how it is affected by the drastic changes in perspective that occur when one grapples with the idea of God.

Johnson illustrates the effect of these perspectival shifts on the lyric subject: In "The Night Watches: III," the experience of living in an anthropocentric reality breaks down and distributes the speaker's sense of self throughout "an aquiline stillness." On one hand, the word "aquiline" suggests a sense of control and possession. On the other, the antonymical ideas of "stillness" and, initially, "rest" connote the idea of surrender. In this desubjectified state, Johnson attempts to trace the origins of human-centered reality but finds something unfathomable at its core. He has investigated the economic and social institutions of this world ("strip mall and steeple alike") and now realizes they are not just means of maintaining the status quo, but are instead "anthems," anthems composed of "recursive / collisions / of / first / word / and / monolith"—a fitting metaphor for competing forms of narcissism. The "un-plumbable" simultaneity of the cosmos and lyric subject in "The Night Watches: IV" illustrates Johnson's essential conundrum: the subject cannot be isolated since it now exists independently of an individual mind or mode of thinking and is thus effectively *indistinguishable* from the World. Johnson does not worry about the ways in which our world-making may lead to solipsism. Nevertheless, this personal disregard for subjectivism has taken on vast proportions, and he identifies *as the universe.*

In "The Night Watches: IX," Johnson visits the "clay- / spoiled / cities" of ancient civilizations and empires that collapsed due to societal failure or natural catastrophe, and which, according to many legends, were destroyed by deities. However, Johnson here approaches these cataclysm myths from a timeless perspective: "Radiant / multitudes / extend / their / gaze," as though panoptically over the whole realm of time. From this lofty height, these ancient myths suggest that people ultimately worship themselves when they bow down before any gods they believe they can control.

There are several ways in which Johnson's poetry might be described as Neo-Surrealist, according to certain elements or paradigms that are present in his work. By examining Neo-Surrealism and the art of the 21st century, readers can gain a deeper understanding of how *The Night Watches* addresses subjective agency in an era whose intercenntenial trauma is felt very keenly, both in the arts and by humanity at large. In 2017, the American Neo-Surrealist poet Andrew Joron authored a collection of poetry entitled *The Absolute Letter,* in which he showcases his acute feeling for sound through a speculative poetics characterized by ambiguous takes on a wide range of subjects, from philosophy to imagined dystopias. Those familiar with Jason Johnson's work may notice similarities between Andrew Joron's brand of Neo-Surrealism and Johnson's own evolution as a poet over the last 15 years. Most artists share a neurosis that oscillates—"sleeps / and / rises / early"—between the fear that the gap between deep reality and experience cannot be bridged, and the fear that bridging the gap will somehow only widen the great gulf between them. Like Joron, however, Johnson believes that "Anything, real or ideal, that undergoes a self-complicating—ultimately musical—form of motion becomes a sign of the processual emergence of the Infinite within the finite." Consequently, Johnson uses *The Night Watches,* carried as it is across "The / bridge / beyond" *by* the

"The / bridge / beyond," to do what Neo-Surrealists do: fulminate against linear modes of thought and language.

In "Anthems for Advent: No. 1," Johnson once again explores the theme of time and memory, but in this instance he does so through the eyes of my deceased maternal grandfather, harnessing language to synchronize the "visitations" of fading memories with the desire to "retrieve" and "retread" the past. At a deep, metaphysical level, Johnson acknowledges the inadequacy of the human mind to process an ever-changing world—one that is always already in the process of being processed. Yet, in "No. 1," Johnson commands the "Un- ceasing memento" to "relent the distance you patrolled" in anticipation of a time "When we resume the dance," suggesting the possibility of not only reliving but continuing a *longue durée* of change and growth. In fact, Johnson uses "No. 1" to equate the apparent powerless agency of individuals with an omniperspectival view of history that extends far beyond human memory: The imagery in the poem includes references to the idea of a distant and forgotten history ("goodbyes / forged from Morse-strobed, rust-locked, gristmill homesteads") as well as those which suggest *prehistoric* times ("drawn skins of winter" and "when antlers write the dust, / when bronze-glazed lightning furrows yawning dusk, / we will redress the wonders of this place, / retrieve the parbent energies, retread / the ladder for aubades' sake").

Johnson's poems convey the idea that all things, both visible and invisible, are interconnected and ultimately share a single identity. Thus, in "No. 9" of "Anthems for Advent," we hear "the spectrumed apparition" speaking of the esemplasticity of existence and non-existence as an example of this unity, of how "The various dead…stranded on a web / of here-and-not-here, of there-and-not-there—stencil / their shrapnel to a single scene…"

As I mentioned previously, we can gain insight into the unusual formal decisions made by Johnson throughout his latest collection by understanding Andrew Joron's perspective on Neo-Surrealism. Flip through Johnson's first book *The Anvil's Children* and you'll discover his poems subtly growing more consistently concentrated and compressed across this body of his work from 2008 to 2015. In *The Night Watches,* Jason Johnson takes this trend even further and, in so doing, achieves a "declining / stars / decrepit / nadir," wresting himself from ceaseless verbiage—the two-dimensional drivel of "shocked-quartz voices." Producing continually self-referential yet continually self-superseding poetry, Johnson's techniques abstract language's endless deferment of meaning in such a way that his work becomes, as Joron puts it in his 2004 essay entitled *Neo-Surrealism; or, the Sun at Night,* "The purest coincidence of system & accident." The visual arrangements that break with conventional linear and sequential patterns of organization, the complex functions and effects of spaces between units of meaning (sentence groups, phrases, or even individual words), the enjambments, the idiosyncratic spellings, the hyphenations, and the neologisms that Johnson employs may pose a difficult challenge for readers, but Johnson's artistic choices can be better situated if one considers Joron's thought regarding the Neo-Surrealist's employment of whatever it takes to allow for myriad aleatoric meanings.

    For all its experimentalism, perhaps the most important aspect of Johnson's book is its Christian mysticism. Even in today's Byzantine times, Johnson meditates on the necessity of surrendering ego and self to God, as well as on the divinity of Jesus. Johnson applies matters like these to contexts that deliberately conflate consolation and desolation. This, of course, is consistent with the ironized position of Johnson's multiple, utterly differentiated subject: there is not merely a sense of comfort in the midst of hardship and suffering, but that which comforts is itself a source of pain and disappointment. The unspeakable absurdity of the non-duality of distress and solace is at once a sublime truth and a cruel joke.

    Johnson sometimes seems to use visual art as inspiration for a kind of poetic ekphrasis. "Hymns from Purgatory: No. 6," for instance, could almost be interpreted as a detailed description of Edvard Munch's *The Scream*, an example of Early Expressionist art. However, he more frequently and more significantly seems to make ekphrastic use of Surrealist and Abstract Expressionist art and artists like Frida Kahlo, Salvador Dalí, or Jackson Pollock, thereby positioning himself well "within" the avant-garde movements of the 20th century. As a case in point, Johnson subverts conventional representation and representational art, much like an action painter from the 1940s and 1950s, in "CV: A Sentence for Pentecost." The poem describes a captivating, haunting, and intense collection of elements that have been brought together forcefully and tightly united, as in a painting. The word "panoply" refers to both a complete suit of armor as well as a grand array of items, and Johnson finds himself coerced or compelled into a "forced out" assembly of these elements, effectively painting a painting or, when given a posthumanistic interpretation, reconstituting himself in numberless different identities. By mediating one artwork/consciousness/self/identity through his own, Johnson displaces the former, suggesting that its elements have only *now* been "fused" together seamlessly; only *now* do they create a cohesive and unified whole, the result of which the poet characterizes as "zeroed for cipher," paradoxically indicating that the encryption process or code of the first "painting" has been reset by his poetics to its original, unencoded form. Johnson then seems to assert that the ability to initialize or deconstruct an artwork (whether metaphorized or not) is evidence that true mastery, including the ability to create an artwork from scratch, has been given an opportunity to thrive: "technique / always / flowers / in the dark." He later mourns the loss of the ability to remain free-spirited ("free / wheeling") as a consequence of being encumbered by repetitive thoughts and emotions ("echo / burdened"), which cause a mark (as from having been "scored with / wheat") to become "a mutilation / stirring in / the wings." Johnson seems to admit to feeling overwhelmed as an artist grappling with the existential problems of artifactualizing, although the line "totality of frogs" suggests that this sense of disorientation may simply be due to a heightened awareness of himself as a heterogeneous subject whose sense of self is kaleidoscopic. The state of continuous change, of something transformative perpetually happening in a sacred space, in which Johnson finds himself ("an altar / where / blood / becomes / amber"), corresponds with Joron's concept of Neo-Surrealism, which he describes in *Neo-Surrealism; or, the Sun at Night* as a state that is "neither natural nor artificial," where language is freed, and an infinite expanse of impossible things lies "brimming beneath the surface of stabilized meaning."

Joron's insights notwithstanding, I can no longer continue my characterization of Johnson as a Neo-Surrealist because of how the poetic imagery of "CV" resolves the issues of endless deferral, concentration by reduction, desubjectification, and devastating implication. In its Pentecostal *enthousiasmós,* the conscious and unconscious, sound and meaning, the real and the imaginary are made radically monistic, that is, their separateness stands neither in contrast nor in contradiction to their coalescence into one. The essence of each lies in its identity both with itself and everything it is not. Thus, Johnson stands revealed as a Noumenist.

Noumenism is a contemporary movement of artistic expression that erases the line between German philosopher Immanuel Kant's concepts of *phenomena* (the known, the perceptible) and *noumena* (the unknowable, the imperceptible). The fusion of these realms opens up a new way of seeing the everyday world, while coinstantaneously aligning with all human experiences of the sacred and the divine. Thus, while it echoes ancient philosophies that do not dissociate the spiritual and the material, Noumenism still offers a fresh perspective, one that pushes the boundaries of art, and defies the conventions of the contemporary art world. Noumenist art acts as a conduit for engagement with the noumenal realm through the medium of aesthetic experience. In Noumenist art, there is a synthesis of ideas and perceptions, enabling one to form a comprehensive aesthetic evaluation of the artwork that is equivalent to one's experience of all its sensory stimuli. Mind-independent reality, sensory perception, and non-perceptual thoughts are encountered simultaneously *as the same thing,* and one is connected to something greater: the *logos* (the unity of opposites; the divine principle that underlies the creation and order of the universe). It hearkens back to Meister Eckhart's theology—"My eye and God's eye are one eye." Therefore, the Christian mystic is as "stupid" as "the stars / may / have / been," persisting in faith in something which is not provable by any empirical or rational means, guarding against the self while simultaneously believing that this self and God are one. Observe Pope John XXII, his head in his hands, trying to understand this unitive consciousness; it cannot be fully grasped as there is no obverse of Eckhartian non-dualism. Thus, by the esoteric principle of "static"—a word Johnson uses to describe the lack of meaning in human communication, as the very "bones" of clear "meaningness"—opacity is transparency, non-being is being, chaos is order, and the Abyss is Paradise itself. The "technic" (order and control) of the artist is "a rage" (frenzied emotion). Flourishing growth is portrayed as irritability, a paradoxical image, and a place for nurturing children is equated with encrypted symbols: even in the quiet peace of "blooming / midnight," the "static" persists, like an "irascible" presence in a "creche of ciphers."

ZANE GILLESPIE, D. M. A.
February 3, 2023
Little Rock Air Force Base, AR

Zane Gillespie is Ecumenical Director of Music at Little Rock Air Force Base in Jacksonville, AR, USA. He has served as Executive Board Member for Music Theory for the Southern Chapter of The College Music Society (2019-2021). As a composer of contemporary classical music, he has written many works. Most recently, his *Metanoia* (for woodwind quintet & fixed-media electronics) was published by Gusthold Music Publishers. As a researcher, Zane has had papers published in peer-reviewed journals such as *Technoetic Arts*, *Cybernetics & Human Knowing*, *College Music Symposium*, and *The Edgar Allan Poe Review*. His current focus is on music composition.
Website: http://zane-gillespie.squarespace.com/
E-mail: rzgllspe@memphisalumni.org

ACKNOWLEDGMENTS

Many of the poems in this collection have appeared in the following publications: *Anglican Theological Review*, *Hieroglyph*, *The Kitchen Poet*, and *New Mystics Online*.

EDITOR'S NOTE

These pages have carefully preserved all the idiosyncrasies (e.g., eccentric spelling and grammar, hyphenated compound words, neologisms, etc.) that are characteristic of the poet, who has thoroughly reviewed all proofs of this book. In "The Night Watches: V.," the word "collect" (pronounced /ˈkälek(t)/) refers to a short prayer, especially one assigned to a particular day or season. "Hymns from Purgatory" begins with "No. 3," because "No. 2" has been lost, and "No. 1" was published as the last poem of Johnson's previous collection *The Anvil's Children*.

THE NIGHT WATCHES

THE NIGHT WATCHES
AN ASCENT

*To
reckon
the
revelation
to*

*stand
flip
in*

*the
face
of*

God

*To
crank*

10,000

*images
to*

*a
chaos*

I.

Our counterparts' deeper pain
is more than a   wisp and an

un-   burdening, but an   un-

ending train of ice   in
an un-   elixired be-   yond

II.

Mix-

ups

like
this
all

the
time

slough

from
our

feet

calcify
and
vanish

in
the
river—

an
offal

ferried
off

III.

At rest—

        and an opening comes

an aquiline stillness casts

        weeds out of the rattling volcano

an ending—not a regretting—

        pours out its hallowed tongues

on strip mall and steeple alike

        on the student's purple hopes

on the mother's pyrrhic joys

IV.

Your
anthems
run
aground

recursive
collisions
of
first

word
and
monolith

birth
un-

plumbable
neon
vaults
of
cosmic
wind

V.

    A minimal burst and
           then the standards
    come. Conflagration after collect—

        All too brief
    the legacy of drums
          like an indictment

          wriggles back to
          the desert into
    a fresh-creped ruin

          where skin subsides
    and buries its chorus
          on the cusp

          of fractal ancestries
          of no account

VI.

Retrieval poises in our wake,
recasts the old disease but
with a difference, a calf
       lilted with alchemy
       belayed like so
       many certainties, like
so many centuries of knowing
       you were wrong
       but still proud
of all the twilights, of
       all the nor'easter
       voyages you wasted

       And for what?
All for a withering chance
in a brown field blight-struck
       and still failing

VII.

    We all rehearse
    the legends of
               the sea,
               a center
        dancers clutch and cling
            to year
            after year—
            those moments
      levers of atonement mow
            our bodies
      down to an hour
      and labor an opening
a stone's throw
        as the crow flies

VIII.

A
gale

takes

root

in
the
mind—

a
memorial
of

un   -   even

light
and
the

un   -   relenting

fragrance
of

men

gasping

but

still

here

IX.

Radiant

multitudes

extend

their

gaze

while

clay-

spoiled

cities

flicker

and

flame

out

X.

A
name

moots

river
and
border

triggers
the

smallest

echo

perfects

the
machine

transfixes

us
roots
us

to
the
spot

routs

regret,

splits

atom
and

drouth

commits

its

cosmic

utterance
to

a
first

combustion

realizes

the
time

sleeps
and

rises

early

XI.

In
the
mountains

an
asylum
identifies

itself
with
the

steaming
streets
of

heaven
teeming
with

goldenrod
and
a

clean
thaw—
      Only

        the
        dead
        know

the
way
out—

Only
they
know

the
meaning
of

kindred
and
cloud

XII.

Even

song

can

only

take

us

so

far

The
bridge

beyond

is

not

ours
but
ours

to
braid
with

palsy
and
mange

with
another

higher

operation
of
mercy

Sigh

if
we

must

Release
if

we

can

Pretend
the
voices

halt

us
in
the

dark

if

all

we

have

left

is

board

bone
and

bread

XIII.

      A great leveler
           comes, stalks
        through a frost-engendered
nuisance of trees, patrols
        the rim,
mans the last checkpoint
     until we say
our goodbyes and set
         our gifts
     at his feet

XIV.

      See —

the emblazoned Christ

the studded chevron

      overwhelms

the umbilical vision

      between

transept and time

between the first

      promise

and the last

XV.

    His

    hammer

        forbids

        us

        ecstasy
        without

        a
        fight

        The
        sheen

        of
        dung

        beetles

        on
        a
        patch

        of
        in
        memoriam

        monstrance-fires —

    His

    intention

    His

    tectonic

    hand

        perturbs
        the

        moon
        and

        the
        wind

        that
        grinds

        down
        mountains

        and
        ruins

    His

    utter

    silence

        stuns

        us

XVI.

The sun emits
  a fresh hell
    all its own
In the woods
  our primal
    parents register in
the gaps a dark
  nuance of loss
    a
pungent
  wolf-skeined synergy
    a
foreign
  pageantry and
    chronicle
of cisterns
  filling
    fast
with family rites
  for no reason
    except to extend
their
  fingers
    toward an
ever-
  shifting
    east

XVII.

A
chrismed

counterpoint
to
calcium-

sickled

cataracts

threads

solitude's

blackest

glove
with
migrations

and
a
subtle

power

brilliant
with
leaves

and
rubble

a
wheel

trembling
in

the
silver

silence

XVIII.

Between
phenomena
a

gleaning

radiance

comes
and
stirs

our

bones
to
a

stillness

a
roof
of

rolling

water
and
no

regret

*The fallacy
that rises
out of
the dark
and calls
to us
sows us
to an
inevitable stillness*

*Angling to
heaven we
plight an
offering for
a retroactive
oath a*

clot-fettered tree

that leans

both forward

and back

ANTHEMS FOR ADVENT

No. 1
In memoriam Thurel Winfield Tutor

Among visitations   and   the drawn   skins of winter,
hard   wedges—   chrome-blue children—   grow,   prolong
their amateur   visions, their   saline   gifts, their   duds,
        last   things   all.

        Un-   ceasing   memento,
lasso your   silken   cloud, your   midnight   purpose,
relent the   distance   you   patrolled, goodbyes
forged from   Morse-strobed, rust-locked, gristmill   homesteads.

    When   we   resume the dance,
     when   antlers   write   the dust,
when bronze-glazed   lightning   furrows yawning dusk,

we   will redress   the wonders of   this place,
retrieve   the parbent   energies, retread
      the ladder for   aubades' sake.

29

No. 2

Phantom specimen,   wild-rabbit tableland
peopled with dirt   and mollusks of every
kind—frontiering   long   sequences,   long waves, long
red-posted doors   to whatever left its trail

       of shit   and venom behind:
       petrified,   centuries dead,
       a permafrosted,   rustic,
       brittle,   seized-up, stoved-in cove-

       nant.   More of the same   withered
hand   haunts us, tails   us, scales   the crystal image
       we raised,   razed, and   raised again

for the sake   of *some thing*,   *some* wind-   trialed stanchion
       from petals   whores   scattered hard-
by, hard-won, hard-wired, from   *some* clay compacted.

No. 3

The space of
      a week's cold
shadows—the pilgrim's
      façade—decants again,
tables discussions again,

      a turbulent still
life bedeviling earth,
      alchemy's armistice broken
with winter again.

      Again we travel
over a murmuring
      field of open
sores. Again fog
      ripens too fast.

No. 4

        Shuttered with questions,
a gathering of
        lean voices fresh
from distant codas
        and gray hinterlands
lashes the sky
        to a frenzy
of belches un-
            fathomed,
    resets the quixotic
        machinery of ciphers—
a dust-rumpled locust
        honey-sheathed hysteria, our
    lint-coated crimson marauder.

No. 5

Our distant witness
whispers to deep on deep
from the final flickering brink of a gray remove.
(an index of ruin,

a dream dropped blind,
a motion sustained in the bones
like a prodigy's wealth and energy spilled
on the bridge between innocence and night)

Unfounded, unmoored, unfeted, unreckoned, almost invisible
Is this primal-driven fancy really a gossamer plunge
and caisson of summer
or just a hinterland of emblazoned echoes,
a contrivance of absolute zero,
and lice-pearled widow's weeds?

No. 6
In memoriam Ray Godwin

1.

Wheeling the trumpets of a thousand shimmering dead,
overwhelming iron devastations
binge flashpoints, sink love
so deep the permafrost begins
to quiver in our last coherent orbit.

2.

This ultimate reckless apogee
negates whatever thrift we had left—,
the Spirit's rhythm and history
of a vanishing war—,

3.

tipping, touching

the powder-keg
breaching with cloud
-shriven icons
              its final malingering

splendor.

No. 7
Thinking of Geoffrey Hill

Rank and wretched state:

worn	out	battling
	on on	fumes
realizing		your
	thunder	wastes
before	chance	
		groundings

knowing your acolytes'

shadows	cast too	far to
	windward	
	zag too	far from

assumption and rest—

Or so the blazing constellation seems
To say in the aftermath of harvest watches.

No. 8

Once sifted

                                                    through these

molten camp

                                                    sites and

salt-foxed effigies,

                                                    we can

only imagine

                                                  the force

that brittled

                                                the humdrum

and wrested

                                                  grace from

a coal-manged

                                                crusty sphinx

No. 9
for the Manchester dead

A velocity of kingdoms in the sun
imparts a presence not entirely ours,
a sophisticated roundabout of sense
demanding fog dissipate like love
beneath a sheltered wound. A wont, a curse
we digitize, archive with a dung-fed blaze,
sooner or later will consecrate the bow,
the spectrumed apparition in the distance.

The various dead who flood the thrones at evening—
like solstice singers stranded on a web
of here-and-not-here, of there-and-not-there—stencil
their shrapnel to a single scene,
                                          a vespers
always flickering, always almost home,
a wilderness of bones who always rise.

No. 10

A reclamation of the dead,
a curt revival in the shadows:

Only the voiceless will balance on the canyon's mouth,
a sting rust-bloodied all too eager in their hips
and lungs—a lunge
from out of nowhere into nothing,
the air just another marrow turn dust,

a silt between the toes in the garden before we know anything,
a series of yawning boughs reaching all places all at once all together,
a bit of ozone clinched in the mind,
a bit held hard in the teeth—.

Every second is always another Jerusalem never redeemed,
always sacked to brands and bellows and ashes,
its borders, another earth always about to be born.

No. 11

Salvage the grief-coat and drink
for a little while from the fog's relentless fist:

Not the bitter after-image,
not a course-hemmed verdure,
not even the bow-slung dream
at the crown's white core,
but the stubborn sound of nations
poor in feeling
aflame with the suet of children.

Only the uterine wreckage of history
can slow it down, can stem
it, this process of carcassing,
a sun-spoiling chaos of sand
and redux of mismorphs to zero.

HYMNS FROM PURGATORY

No. 3

1.
Signals sleep in the mountain's braided web,
a rift that logics and creeds cannot cross—.
Not even the elect—whose work
is shepherding law through the incense of history—
can rise through the silent plume of the absolute,
a point where song and scab
plateau into a veneer of grief and symmetry.

2.
Equations scatter their names—
the shocked-quartz voices of children,
their sleeves of neon velvet and trickling glass,
hands opening a dove's balmed anthem,
hanging a bow in the sky—
over a pearl-spun Atlantic
filthed by the debris of a dream.

No. 4

1.

The watchman laces his sentence with the ciphers of winter,
Merging the remains of elders with the shadows of ballasts'
Beacon-belled beds. His solemn habits speed vessels—
Bellies hooked and cranked, marbled and thorned,
The circulations of a buckled sky,
A country's proof of absent name-rubbed nails—
Through the softened star-roads blind men thrust into pockets.

2.

Phantom navigations stir
sinews
of bough-prone gates

to a spurt of glands
and a stiffened keel-horned
arc.

3.

not yet the shock of sin
a lice-rimmed sex

not yet the garden's footing
a spilt connection

not yet the desert well
a puppet seed

4.

The unction
a spatter-stone,
a vanishing shroud.

No. 5
written on the Feast of the Visitation

1.

The	warm	soul
of		words
and the	tripwire	epiphany
	it brings—	
a silver		manifestation
of	angel	bones
and	nimbus	
	wings	
our	mothers	knit
out of silence and		dead
men's	dreams	

2.

Combusted
viscera

a
cosmic
suet
loomed
and
wracked
on
clotted
leaves

a
badge
of
un-

christened
privates

3.

Sleeping

Steerage

In
The
Bosom

Of
A
Reluctant

Fire—
We

Nurse

(*in*

communicado)

Rolled-
Back
Stones

And
Sputtering
Stars

No. 6

1.
The boat we tell to the distance,
a weather heaved up like slop to the moon,
must take its chances
in this village of paper houses and suicides.

2.
Whether we tell it right or not won't bilge its marble keel,
our warning faint—
the sheep few in the hold, so many leaves
a solemn leaden sponge.

Submit or adjust, *still*
its ribs will clot to bursting.

3.
Fixed, defunct, *un*troubled—
an impasse of air,
                        a twice-sexed traffic of snow.

No. 7

                                                Look on the hoisted blaze

1.

A   wound   hulled out
by   fever

        the ever-sharpening
                            crown
of   Babeled
        thorns

                            on the floor where children gather

2.

The realization of stars

        wax   wings

for the dead   for the mass

        for a   meal

                          timber under a silk-draped iron station

3.

                Fields

of   Icharas   root

        anonymous   twilight.

        Brother:

        call
for the   cripple's
        onused

        hymn

                                a bitter visitation

4.

       Triggering   the assumption

of   twinned   labors—
the   column   and the spear—

the hinges of   transfigured thunder
quarter   unpalatable

                        scrys
       studded
with   the blood
of   flood-filthed   smithies

and the   shit
of   stubborn   stars—

                    the   asymptotes

of   murder and   thin   air

                                    cut from the ash and bone

5.

To   outlive   the   boundary
and   hang
in the ecstasy   of   shadows

                                  of a pregnant grave

No. 8

                                                                   The pasts our mothers soften

1.

```
My father      spoke                           of      manhood
as an          alloy
               conjured
                                               by
the            collision                       of
                                                        violence
               and
                                                        memory.
```

                                         a bridge between here

2.

```
Feast on       the bowl                of      black        wings
before         the periphery   of      dusk
turns          the house               to      flames.
```

                                         and the plains

3.

```
We haul        fish                            from
the                                                     ruins
                                               of       joy

but the hills  won't have it
or             the buildup and thaw of         wreckage

in the         shallows                        of       summer.
```

                                       where our children dream

4.

The last scene   of   faith
            moment   of   nakedness
        straddling the station   for   thunder's
sake   the   for   womb's.

frolic and frost

5.

Reluctance of fog   we have worn   your   tarnish enough.

We   have   loved your   transience in our   mouths each morning.

But   now   it   is   time to let   go,

pour lye   in the river and wine in the   bull's open   wound.

but die in the snow

No. 9

      I.

1.

Let

Combines

Echo

Straightway

The
Daisies
Of

Remembrance

With

A
Pall
Of

Angel-

Weeds

2.

Comet-

Threaded

Travelers

Patrol

Nimbus-

Clotted

Towns

For
Seedless
Women

For
Unpaled
Moss-

Gimped

Fences

3.

On
The
Virginal

Periphery

Moth-
Gagged
Mag-

Pie
Prison-
Meat

Wrestle

With
Seraph-
Haired

Salve-
Enforced
Marauders

Whose
Only
Vision

Is

An
Array
Of

Aluminum

Christs

Telescoped

From
Turn-

Pike
To

Mesa
And

Hatteras-

Ward

Again

II.

1.

Flames

Of
A
Billowing

Law

Veins

Of
A
Bridgeless

Morning—

A
Tender

Drifting

Differential
Of

Winter

2.

Sycamore—

        A
       Motive
         In
       Three

Rooms

3.

The   Revelations

Of
Unstunted

Siblings

Unbuckle

Us

From
Cancer
And
Frost

And
From
The

Perennial

Penwheeled

Worm's

Intentions

4.

Thunderscapes—

An
Un-

Digested

Mimicry
And
Ransom:

Your
Ministry
Is

The

Pill-

Bug

And

The

Moon

The

Calculus

Of

Gravity

And

The

Dog's

Dander—

CV
A SENTENCE FOR PENTECOST

Ever-
roving
aluminum-
succored

costly and honey-

headed
nimbus-
tuckered
child

manhole for none

such
pubic
curtailment
rendered

light in mime

scorch the shield-

bloated

hatch with egg-

blossoms

this all-too

ignorance

nevers the

chum

away a

panoply

forced out and fused

zeroed for cipher

technique
always
flowers

in the dark

before noose-

tide

shakes its

alms

to the root

a bitter-not-knowing

snowmelt

alls the simmer

and gypsum with

well-
pangs

borne down on

our
last
good

cry before convulsive

we
shrive
too
much
we
bare
too

much and never

really
enough
free
wheeling
echo
burdened

scored with

wheat

a mutilation

stirring in

the wings the

totality of frogs

here and a

bit
yonder
we
minister

in the blood

the lax

perversion that blows

through these towns

like

dross before fire

large
unwieldy

bubbles of beveled

glass
real

presence of shock

and awe

this sheath a

rose

partitions the

wound from

a muse

too

terrible to think

it
could
ever
coil
again
ever
rise
again
hitch
your

scars to one

moment

then another

then another

before the rattle

clutches
your
throat
no
two
children
will

jesus the same

way
twice

the bone-

shirt

bears up for

nothing

like

years a wheel

our
sisters'

find on the

scrap
heap
sour-toothed
liver-edged
firecade
just
one
way

to address the

boils and scratch

in the yard

on notice a

swatch in the kiln

some
sourceless
voice

out of the east

some

breath that shapes

the flares of

morning to highways

rivers that haunt

pneumatic
flesh
always

quiver the board

an altar

where
blood
becomes
amber

a law a

crystal

ball a

prophet's

call a

lightning
mountain

booth for three

no
waiting

there is

no
cure-all

like this anywhere

a rebel

hanging by the thread

of day a

pilgrimage
descent

through nascent

clay
his

voice a

contest of

declining
stars
decrepit
nadir

and dog-

rot
know
more

than the slick

of air

sanded
craters

layer up desert

fires
golden
tels

streaked with forge

dust
fused

zeroed for semper

this reversal a

competence of rain

stirs
our
visceral
dream

to a mist-

shorn
maudlin
descant

stupid though the stars

may
have
been

the gong

still
levels
their

madness to a

pulse and caw

a wayward

sprit a

rudder
dregged

away this sheath

of egg-

blossoms'
convulsive
never-enough

short

shrinks and last

peals of

winter an

alive-like
thing

foment of recognitions

thin

places from the outset

this struggle

of traffic and

swim by numbers

this magenta

image

speaking with wired

jaw a godless

world
wander

mumble out of mind

out of time

static
determines
our
bones
flames
our
meaningness
our

technic a rage

and blooming

mid-
night

an irascible

creche of ciphers

A NOTE ABOUT THE AUTHOR

Jason W. Johnson is an Assistant Professor in the Department of English at Guilford Technical Community College in Jamestown, NC, USA. Since 2019, he has served as President of the Board of Directors of The Friendship Table, a nonprofit organization committed to alleviating food insecurity. His published work includes "Historical and Political Poems" in *Reading William Gilmore Simms: Essays of Introduction to the Author's Canon* (Columbia, SC: University of South Carolina Press, 2017) and much original poetry, including the collection *The Anvil's Children* (Oxford, MS: VOX Press, 2015). At present, he is primarily concentrating on writing poetry.

E-mail: jwjohns1@gmail.com

A NOTE ABOUT THE TYPE

The text of this book was set in Electra, a typeface designed by W. A. Dwiggins (1880-1956). This face cannot be classified as either modern or old style as it is not based on any historical model and does not resemble any particular period or style. Unlike most modern faces, it avoids the stark contrast between thick and thin elements, thus conveying a sense of uninterrupted flow and potency.

Printed and bound by BookBaby, Pennsauken, New Jersey
Designed by Zane Gillespie